Play It Safe!

by Cindy Chapman

Reading Consultant: Wiley Blevins, M.A.
Phonics/Early Reading Specialist

 COMPASS POINT BOOKS

Minneapolis, Minnesota

Compass Point Books
3109 West 50th Street, #115
Minneapolis, MN 55410

Visit Compass Point Books on the Internet at *www.compasspointbooks.com*
or e-mail your request to *custserv@compasspointbooks.com*

Photographs ©: Cover and p. 1: Capstone Press/Gary Sundermeyer, p. 6: Capstone Press/Gary
Sundermeyer, p. 7: Capstone Press/Gary Sundermeyer, p. 8: Corbis/LWA-Sharie Kennedy,
p. 9: Corbis/Layne Kennedy at CLM, p. 10: Index Stock Imagery/Kindra Clineff, p. 11: Ann
and Rob Simpson, p. 12: top left: Index Stock Imagery/Bob Winsett, p. 12: bottom right: Corbis

Editorial Development: Alice Dickstein, Alice Boynton
Photo Researcher: Wanda Winch
Design/Page Production: Silver Editions, Inc.

Library of Congress Cataloging-in-Publication Data
Chapman, Cindy.
  Play it safe! / by Cindy Chapman.
     p. cm. — (Compass Point phonics readers)
Summary: Discusses how to keep safe while playing outdoors in
easy-to-read text that incorporates phonics instruction and rebuses.
Includes bibliographical references (p. 16) and index.
  ISBN 0-7565-0520-8 (alk. paper)
  1. Outdoor recreation for children—Safety measures—Juvenile
literature. 2. Play—Safety measures—-Juvenile literature. 3.
Reading—Phonetic method—Juvenile literature. [1. Outdoor
recreation—Safety measures. 2. Play—Safety measures. 3. Safety. 4.
Reading—Phonetic method. 5. Rebuses.] I. Title. II. Series.
  GV191.625.C53 2003
  796.5'028'9—dc21   2003006365

Table of Contents

Dear Parent or Caregiver,

Welcome to Compass Point Phonics Readers, books of information for young children. Each book concentrates on specific phonic sounds and words commonly found in beginning reading materials. Featuring eye-catching photographs, every book explores a single science or social studies concept that is sure to grab a child's interest.

So snuggle up with your child, and let's begin. Start by reading aloud the Mother Goose nursery rhyme on the next page. As you read, stress the words in dark type. These are the words that contain the phonic sounds featured in this book. After several readings, pause before the rhyming words, and let your child chime in.

Now let's read *Play It Safe!* If your child is a beginning reader, have him or her first read it silently. Then ask your child to read it aloud. For children who are not yet reading, read the book aloud as you run your finger under the words. Ask your child to imitate, or "echo," what he or she has just heard.

Discussing the book's content with your child:
Explain to your child that everyone has a responsibility to follow rules. Rules help people work and play safely. They also help us work and play in a way that is fair.

At the back of the book is a fun Word Bingo game. Your child will take pride in demonstrating his or her mastery of the phonic sounds and the high-frequency words.

Enjoy Compass Point Phonics Readers and watch your child read and learn!

How Many Days

How many **days** has my baby to **play?**
Saturday, Sunday, Monday,
Tuesday, Wednesday, Thursday, Friday,
Saturday, Sunday, Monday.
Hop **away,** skip **away,**
My baby wants to **play,**
My baby wants to **play** every **day.**

A  pool can be fun.
You may swim!
You may splash!

But play it safe!
Wait and do not run.
Stay safe and take turns.

A  playground can be lots of fun.
You may slide!
You may ride!

But play it safe!
Look out!
Stay safe and do not get
in the way.

A  beach can be fun in the sun.
You may fish.
You may fill a pail with shells.

But play it safe!
Obey the rules.
Stay safe and do not go far.

These kids play it safe.
Tell how.

Word List

Long *a (ai, ay)*

ai
pail
wait

ay
may
play
stay
way

Digraph *sh*
fish
shells
splash

High-Frequency
far
how

Social Studies
obey
rules
take turns

Word Bingo

You will need:
- 1 sheet of paper
- 18 game pieces, such as pennies, beans, or checkers

Player 1

play	stay	wait
pail	fish	train
shells	way	how

How to Play

- Fold and cut a sheet of paper into 12 pieces. Write each game word on one of the pieces. The words are *day, far, fish, how, may, pail, play, shells, stay, train, wait, way.*
- Fold each piece of paper and put it in a bag or box.
- The players take turns picking a folded paper and reading the word aloud. Each player then covers the word if it appears on his or her game card. The first player to cover 3 words either down, across, or on the diagonal wins. You can also play until the whole card is covered.

Player 2

fish	day	shells
how	stay	wait
play	may	far

Read More

Bizley, Kirk. *Swimming*. You Can Do It! Series. Chicago, Ill.: Heinemann Library, 2000.

Hill, Mary. *Signs at the Pool*. Welcome Books Series. New York: Children's Press, 2003.

Royston, Angela. *Safety First*. Safe and Sound Series. Des Plaines, Ill.: Heinemann Library, 2000.

Schultz, Kathy. *Always Be Safe*. Rookie Readers Series. New York: Children's Press, 2003.

Index